HORNS
and
ANTLERS

BY WILFRID S. BRONSON

Illustrated by the Author

SUNSTONE
PRESS

SANTA FE

Sunstone books may be purchased for educational, business, or sales promotional use.
For information please write: Special Markets Department, Sunstone Press,
P.O. Box 2321, Santa Fe, New Mexico 87504-2321.

Printed on acid-free paper

Library of Congress Cataloging-in-Publication Data

Bronson, Wilfrid S. (Wilfrid Swancourt), 1894-1985.
  Horns and antlers / written and illustrated by Wilfrid Swancourt Bronson.
    pages cm
  Originally published: New York : Harcourt, Brace and Company, 1942.
  ISBN 978-0-86534-914-8 (softcover : alkaline paper)
  1. Deer--North America. 2. Elk--North America. 3. Antelopes--North America.
I. Title.
  QL737.U5B94 2013
  599.65--dc23
                              2013012927

WWW.SUNSTONEPRESS.COM
SUNSTONE PRESS / POST OFFICE BOX 2321 / SANTA FE, NM 87504-2321 /USA
(505) 988-4418 / ORDERS ONLY (800) 243-5644 / FAX (505) 988-1025

CONTENTS

HORNS AND ANTLERS

I'LL give you something to put in your book," said the old deer hunter. He took the corn-cob from between his teeth, pursed his lips, and blew a long row of smoke rings. Then, as though reading his own indoor skywriting, he made a soft but resonant, almost dovelike sound. "Oo-hrroo-oo-ooh."

"Most everybody thinks that's the call of a

hoot owl," he said, looking wise. "Well, it ain't. It's made by a white-tailed deer." I told him I had often heard it in the woods at night, sometimes from several directions at once. "I always thought," I said, trying to be tactful, "that it was a family of owls calling back and forth."

"Nope, it's a family of deer, most likely a doe keepin' track of her two fawns while they browse." This was all very interesting, but all very wrong. A whitetail fawn sometimes calls to its mother with a gentle bleat. Its big sensitive ears easily catch the soft murmur of her answer. A doe may blat like a calf if wounded. Bucks snort and whistle. But no sound made by Virginia or white-tailed deer is at all like the hooting of the Virginia or great horned owl. For the most part deer are silent creatures, making only the rarest use of their voices. Though their sight is not of the best, undoubtedly when feeding at night whitetails easily keep track of each other through their extremely sharp sense of hearing, as well as with a very keen sense of smell.

My old hunter's misinformation was the more surprising because he rarely failed to "get his deer." Maybe in the early morning darkness he kept so still, watching deer trails, that even the owls never noticed him, and their cozy conversations put the deer off guard. But his success in spite of his mistaken notion shows how careful one must be when gathering facts for a book about wild animals.

The old fellow meant to be helpful when he offered me this nonsense about the noises of deer. But how unfortunate it would be to accept it as truth, and retell it in a book to be read and believed by thousands for generations to come! One learns to check and double-check one informant's words against another's and against one's own observations.

So, in this book, before we begin to consider special kinds of deer and antelope, let us take the trouble first to get our facts straight about deer and antelope in general, and the great group of animals to which they belong. It is the group known as bovine or ox-like animals, containing all the cattle and their relatives, the sheep, goats, antelopes, and every type of deer the wide world over. Its members, though of many different kinds, all walk on cloven hoofs and chew the cud, or ruminate, which makes them ruminants.

Now nature is very complicated, and some animals seem to belong in certain groups, yet may have so many peculiar characteristics that they have to be put into a group of their own, in a class by themselves. This is the case with camels which, though their hoofs are cloven in a sense, and though they chew the cud, are too different in too many ways to be true ruminants. And pigs, while having cloven hoofs, do not chew the cud at all. So they most certainly aren't members of the bovine group. Neither pig nor camel can belong to the Society of Cloven-hoofed Cud-chewers.

True ruminants of one or many kinds live in almost every region of the habitable globe. Wherever there is dust or mud or snow enough, sooner or later you will find their footprints. On the heights of snow-capped mountains, in the muck of dankest swamps, in jungle and forest, on grassy plains or driest desert, from the shores of the Arctic Ocean to the Equator, and through all the lands to southward, the signs are there, in the wilderness or in the barnyard. Whoever goes beyond the limits of a town can see, pressed into the earth, the seal of their society. If not the tracks of deer and antelope, wild goats and sheep

7

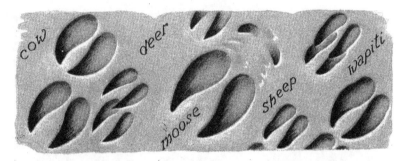

and buffalo, then certainly the impress from the feet of farmers' goats and sheep and cattle.

Something which sets a ruminant apart from other animals cannot be seen by looking at a living chewer of the cud, but is there for all that, and very important to its way of life. This is its stomach, peculiar in being divided into four compartments. Each of these compartments in its turn does a share of digesting the leaves and grass and other plants the creature eats. The first compartment is much larger than the other three, and serves as market basket only. The feeding animal collects food in it, cropping the vegetation steadily, chewing none of it, but swallowing every now and then. Each swallowed

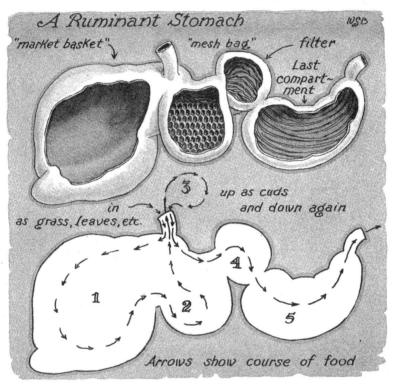

A Ruminant Stomach — WSB

"market basket" — "mesh bag" — filter — Last compartment

in as grass, leaves, etc. — 3 up as cuds and down again

Arrows show course of food

batch of greenery slides down the throat and into the big compartment until the latter is satisfyingly full.

The second compartment is much smaller, a bag or pocket working with the first. It's funny to think how the market basket and the pocket must work always together. This pocket portion

9

is a mesh-bag of a sort, its inside being lined with a mesh-like skin from which comes moisture to soften the collected food.

Now the ruminating starts. Generally the animal lies down. And presently the swallowed batches of food, now well moistened balls, re-

turn to its mouth one by one for careful chewing. These are the cuds. When a cud, well chewed, is swallowed the second time, it slips past the second compartment, filtering through the third into the fourth where true digestion then takes place. Hardly is it swallowed and out of the way, than the next cud rises to be chewed.

Perhaps sometime you can watch a cow. She will chew a while, then swallow and pause. In a jiffy a ripple runs up her throat and she resumes her chewing. The next cud is in her mouth. This is ruminating.

Ruminating is a safety device, not necessary to tame chewers of the cud which can browse or graze all day in open pastures unafraid, but very useful to their wilder kith and kin. To be able to collect one's food as rapidly as possible and then retire to some good hiding place to chew it all in peace and comparative security is important to animals which may be preyed upon by hunters, wolves, wildcats, and so on.

It is certain that ability to chew the cud was acquired by the ancestors of all ruminants from their everlasting need to avoid being seen by enemies. Likewise, for the sake of greater speed in fleeing from danger, the cloven hoofs were developed from the slower five-toed feet of the earlier ancestors. Hoofs are nothing but en-

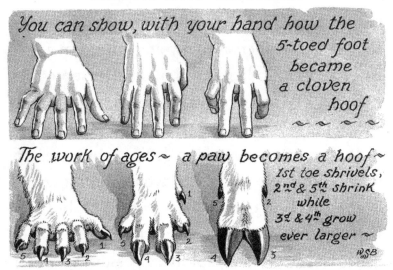

You can show, with your hand how the 5-toed foot became a cloven hoof

The work of ages ~ a paw becomes a hoof ~ 1st toe shrivels, 2nd & 5th shrink while 3d & 4th grow ever larger ~

larged toenails, and on the feet of ruminants, as ages passed, the nails of their third and fourth toes gradually enlarged, while the second and fifth toes shrank to a position up behind them, and the first toe, or thumb, shriveled entirely away. The hard hoofs, sharp edged and pointed, often prove good striking weapons in emergencies, such as when a deer is brought to bay by dogs or wolves or a bear. With a lucky stroke of its far too delicate-looking forefoot, a deer can crack the skull of a wolf and lay him low.

12

Besides market basket stomachs and fast-running, hard-hitting feet, many kinds of ruminants have developed weapons on their heads as well, and great is the variety. There are two main types: horns, worn by antelopes, goats, sheep, and cattle, and antlers, borne by the various kinds of deer. Though similar, horns and antlers have very definite differences. You would never refer to the antlers of a cow. It is just as incorrect to speak of the horns of a deer.

For unlike horns, which grow throughout the whole life of the beast that bears them, antlers are shed and regrown once a year by every deer that wears them. Yet these two types of headgear are not so unlike, in a number of ways, as this might make it seem. Both serve the same purpose—as spears and shields, and possibly as ornaments to be admired. Certainly their spunky owners often act as though quite proud of them. And both are made of nothing else but skin and bone.

For horn is but an altered form of skin, growing always out of skin, just as fingernails and claws and hoofs do, and beaks and feathers of birds, the scales of fishes and reptiles, the shells of turtles, and the hair of mammals such as ruminants and ourselves. All these things are made of horn, as are calluses on the hands of men who work at heavy toil. Calluses come because of wear, a horny protection for the flesh beneath, as nails are a protection for the fingers. Hoofs are simply greater thickenings of horn or nail to protect the toes that run upon the hard, rough ground.

The word "horn" itself has an ancestor, the old-time Latin word "cornu" which means the very same thing. When calluses grow on toes from too much wear, we call them corns, from that old word, but we could say horns as rightly. For horn is what they're made of. The rhinoceros, a three-toed hoofer, distant relative of horses, has a horn on his nose, made of hard,

strong hairs all grown together like the waxed tips of some man's grand mustachios. Thus we see that horn grows from the skin in many forms according to what the need may be.

Horns are hollow and would be scarcely strong enough for use as weapons were they not reinforced within by bony braces. They develop in this way. From two knobs on the skull of an infant ruminant slowly rise two towers of bone. At the same time, from skin surrounding the knobs, grows horn, completely covering the bone. Lengthening steadily, these growths become like two bone daggers in their tightly fitting sheaths of horn. These bone dagger braces will stop growing after a while, but the horny sheaths are likely to continue, fashioning the forms of horns, fancy or plain, of every kind of cow or buffalo or goat or sheep or antelope. In this case, of course, the permanent horny sheaths themselves are actually the weapons of their wearers.

On the other hand, the inner daggers on the heads of deer become the weapons as they grow, often branching into many-pointed spears of solid bone. For with deer the outer covering is very temporary, the sheaths of antlers being but a covering of velvet-haired skin which remains only till the work of weapon-making is complete. While this is going on, from very early spring until later summer, the deer and his antlers are said to be "in velvet" because of these skin sheaths with their plush of short outstanding hairs.

The antlers in these months are very tender, being full of sensitive nerves with which they feel every twig they touch in the tanglewood.

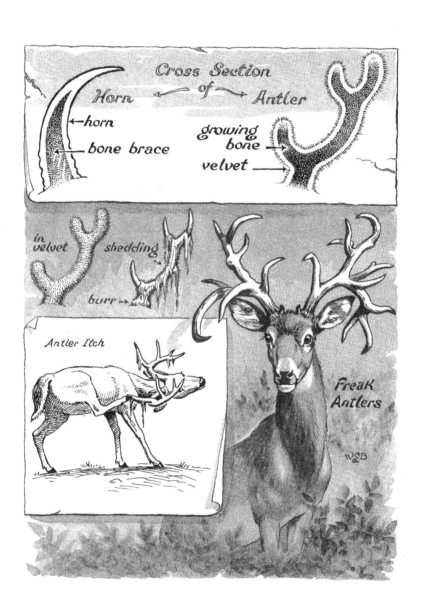

Cross Section

Horn *of* Antler

horn

bone brace

growing bone

velvet

in velvet

shedding

burr

Antler Itch

Freak Antlers

WSB

They are easily injured now, and their owner must move carefully or risk deforming them, a poor preparation for the mating season.

Wherever they are bruised or caused to bleed, uncouth knobs and even extra points may grow in various directions, making a set both badly balanced and unbeautiful. Sometimes if the buck injures his body, not the antlers themselves, they fail to grow well on the side where he was wounded. In the world of trees and brush and rocks through which he often rushes, it is a wonder any deer succeeds in raising a really good and regular rack. But many do.

While developing, the antlers are almost feverishly warm from all the busy blood vessels beneath the velvet, which are building up the bone like masons hurrying to finish a tower within a scaffolding which grows as the tower grows. Once the work is done, the scaffolding comes down. And this is just what happens to the velvet when the antlers are full grown.

A hard, tight ring or burr of bone forms right around the bases of the finished antlers, slowly cutting off the blood supply. While the nerves are still alive, this slowing must create a case of constant antler itch. At any rate the deer often turns his head and, with one sharp hinder hoof, deftly chisels at the velvet, somewhat like a person who can't control the urge to scratch mosquito bites, and endures a little hurt for the relief the scratching brings.

But the nerves do die and the now unfeeling bone dries strong and hard. The velvet skin dries too and peels away, hanging in shreds like Spanish moss on the branches of a tree. The deer helps the process, rubbing his new antlers on shrubbery and saplings, polishing the points well.

Now, newly armed, he is ready and eager to fight every rival for the favor of as many females as he can find. He will wear his weapons through the great fall tournament, battling other bucks, proving which are fittest, which shall win the does and be the fathers of the next year's fawns. By December all pugnacious feelings have disappeared. The struggles are over and done before deep winter settles down. All is harmony again as deer of all ages, bucks, does, and half-grown fawns, gather in herds to live the cold months through.

For a while the bucks retain their splendid crowns. But the antlers are only less temporary than the velvet with which they once were covered. Before spring they are shed in the snow, where mice and squirrels and porcupines enjoy gnawing on them. Within a month new antlers will begin to grow. A young buck which had but two plain spikes his second season and did no fighting with his elders, will, like a tree, add branches every year, until at seven or eight he is in his prime and wears a glorious rack of many points. For a few fall tournaments he can vanquish almost any older buck or younger buck he meets. He has his time of splendor. But after that his antlers grow more feebly every season till, as with all wild things when their powers fail, he falls a prey to some strong enemy.

Quite otherwise with the wearers of horns; the aging bull or ram or goat or antelope still wears its weapons when it dies. For, unlike antlers, horns keep growing and adding something year by year. For the first few years the rate is rapid. But the amount is ever less as the years increase till finally little more horn grows from the bases than will replace that worn off at the tips. And never are they sensitive like antlers in the velvet. Before the horns sprout, calves, kids,

and lambs butt furiously in imitation battles. As their weapons grow, they keep right at it, learning to butt, hook, jab, and parry with increasing skill, and never a tender spell to stop their practice.

Another way in which horns and antlers differ is that though the latter often branch, the former never do. Antlers come in different designs, some as simple spikes, some as large flat areas with points on their edges like the fingers of an open hand, and others in various styles of branching. But all the beautiful variety in horn designs is achieved by widening or lengthening, curving and recurving in C's and S's, long sweeps or sudden, by flattening or rounding, knobbing and notching, wrinkling and ridging, twisting and spiraling. The horns of rams circle outward; those of goats may corkscrew either out or in. Some antelope horns twist near the head and then run straight out to the points. Some spiral all the way. Many bend back but some

curve forward.

Among people there are always some who can't make up their minds just what they want to be, or who can't seem to live according to the rules that others live by. This is true in animal society as well. Among American ruminants the prongbuck antelopes are some of these which make exceptions of themselves. They annually shed their horns (which, antler-like, have one prong or branch) and grow new ones to cover the bony spikes still standing on their heads. Thus they waver in their habits as to headgear, which is like a link between true horns and antlers with some of the features of each.

Nevertheless, prongbucks are like most other cloven-hoofed cud-chewers in many ways: their mouths are minus front teeth in the upper jaw; they commonly live in herds, but the females usually go off by themselves to bear their young; the herds generally divide into groups of males and females for a time each year; and though the males fight among themselves, all battle outside enemies only as a last resort, preferring to run away whenever possible.

As a matter of fact, it looks as though horns and antlers are carried by male ruminants chiefly for duels with others of their own particular breeds. If they were meant for fighting off the beasts of prey, why wouldn't the females need better weapons than the males? It is their double duty to take care not only of themselves but of the precious and defenseless young. Only one kind of female deer, the reindeer or caribou, has any antlers. Some antelope, sheep, and goat females never have horns, and the kinds which have them are often equipped with far less fancy outfits than the males. Apparently the excess armament is primarily for bouts of bull to bull, buck to buck, billy to billy, and ram to ram. This seems almost certain when we remember that buck deer cannot use their antlers till these are full grown, and lose them again in three or four months. Eight months of the year they depend on fleeing or fighting with their feet, as do the does.

As I have pointed out, cloven-hoofed cud-chewers live in every land. We have here in America some native and some imported kinds. Of hollow horns, all kinds of barnyard cattle, goats, and sheep were brought here from the Old World in Colonial times. Our native cattle are the bison and musk-ox; and we have mountain or bighorn sheep. Most antelopes live in Africa or Asia, but we have two kinds in the New World—the prongbucks and the so-called mountain goats.

Many types of deer are found in Europe and in Asia, but our own antler bearers—the moose, wapiti, caribou, mule deer, and whitetails—are the equal in size, beauty, and interesting ways of any deer anywhere else on earth. So from this point forward we are going to have a good long look into the lives of North American deer and antelope.

WHITETAILS — AMERICA'S
FINEST

FIRST let us get acquainted with the whitetails whose portraits I have painted in two
of the color plates. These beautiful animals are a soft red tan in summer and a gray-
brown pepper-and-salt in winter time. All
through the year they wear a white patch on the

throat, white across the nose, around the eyes, inside the ears, inside each leg, and underneath the tail, plus a black spot each side of the chin. Fawns are orange-brown with white spots till, losing their spots when four months old, they don their first fall pepper-and-salt. Because of a slaty quality in this winter coat, deer so attired are said by woodsmen to be "in the blue."

Some of these deer live in nearly every kind of country that America provides, their size and color varying with the many different climates they encounter. Whitetails are paler in the west except in the very wet woods of Washington and Oregon, where they are dark and more like those in the moist forests of the south. These darker deer are also smaller than their brothers of the east and north. In the dry southwest and Mexico, whitetails are very small indeed, some adults weighing scarcely thirty pounds. Of whitetail bucks in Canada and in our northern and eastern states, the average stands some three and one half feet at the shoulder, and weighs about two hundred pounds. Many are smaller, but some are big enough to weigh three hundred pounds, and the record whitetail buck was over nine and one half feet from his nose to tail-tip, and weighed a full four hundred.

In many ways these are the most advanced and finest of American deer. Mule deer, most nearly like them, average just a little heavier and, to many westerners who know them best, mule deer antlers may seem more magnificent. The latter is, however, a matter of taste alone. If you like antlers that branch and branch again, you'll say the mule deer takes the prize. If you prefer a pair of beams from which all branches rise, you'll hand the trophy to the whitetail. Such matters cannot be disputed. But neither can it be denied that in most other ways, the whitetail really does excel.

The whitetail takes first prize for speed. On the straightaway he has a wide edge on the mule deer. Though the latter, with his very special bounding gait can clear wide chasms and climb rocky hills with almost floating ease, on more even land he just isn't in it. Here he tires very soon when pressed. For a short distance he may match a sprinting whitetail at some forty miles per hour, but is quite unable to sustain the cruising speed of thirty miles or more per hour which the whitetail can keep up for three or four miles without flagging. One American ruminant only can outrun the whitetail, and that's the prongbuck antelope of the open plains and deserts.

The whitetail's moves are lightning fast when danger comes upon him suddenly. There's no bewildered, often fatal pause of confusion like the mule deer's before he gets out of an enemy's way. And besides being so swift of action, the whitetail is the wiliest, most elusive of all deer, having a bigger box of tricks to play on his pursuers than any other. He has no fear of ordinary hounds, dawdling along before them, using as

many ruses as a fox, skulking through brush, wading in streams to spoil the scent, swimming lakes, or simply circling back to his own tracks behind the dogs till he has led them in a loop. Then, leaping over a log perhaps, to land some ten or fifteen feet away, he runs a little way downwind and rests while the whining dogs must waste much time and power running in circles. The change in their tone tells him the instant they find the trail again, and fresh as a daisy he spurts away to try new tricks with the

not so happy hullabaloo of the tiring hounds behind him. But if really put to it, he'll swim a
lake or river with the greatest ease.

Another side of the whitetail's intelligence is
shown in his great adaptability. He has his pref-
erences, but has learned to live in almost every
climate and condition in this country. Though
principally a forest dweller, his kind was common in big herds upon the open prairies of the
south and midwest back in pioneering days.
Whitetails love the wooded and well-watered
hills, but get along quite well among the brush
and willows by creeks in drier and more level
land. They haunt the swamps of Florida and
manage in the cold of Canada, flourish in the far
southwest and arid Mexico. In fact, some may
be found in almost every state save California,
often overlapping, as they do, the ranges of the
more restricted mule deer. They are represented
through all of Central America, clear into the
jungles and mountains of northern South Amer-

ica.

Theirs is the only breed of deer that has increased its range since America was settled,
actually following farmers into regions where
whitetails had never been before. Instead of giving ground before the white men advancing
through their wilderness with ax and gun, they
kept close to the new clearings and helped themselves to the strange, delightful vegetables
planted there. At night they jumped rail fences
with the utmost ease, growing fat and strong on
"stolen sweets," even as they sometimes raid the
gardens of today. Of course, with the most efficient firearms in the hands of millions of hunters, they would not last long without protection
of the law. But because they have it, there are
probably more whitetails at the present time
than ever before.

Of the noises the strangers made, the whitetails soon could tell the difference between those
that spoke of trouble and those that implied no

harm. The footfall of the hunter was as old as Indians to them, but the explosion of gunpowder was something utterly new and terrifying. Yet the screech of sawmills did not frighten them away, nor the scream of a locomotive's whistle, nor its hiss and chug, nor its roar and rumble, nor its bell. The sounds of factory and farm were soon accepted as not threatening.

Indeed, so confident do these deer become when not too often disturbed that, though normally feeding by night and close to cover, they are sometimes seen in broad daylight far from the forest, out in the pastures nibbling weeds beside their big grass-cropping relatives, the cows. Being browsers, they prefer leafy weeds to grass, and so may even improve the farmer's fields by feeding there. If we could teach our dogs not to molest them, they might be seen upon suburban lawns, right in our towns.

In still another way whitetails could be called foremost of American deer. Besides being com-

monest in the country as a whole, they were the first deer the early colonists encountered. That is why they are often called Virginian or Virginia deer. Sir Walter Raleigh, writing of experiences in America way back in 1584, gave them this name since he first saw them in Virginia. Farther north the Pilgrims found them too, and fortunate they were. For just as the deer provided food, clothes, and tepee coverings for Indians, they helped to feed and clothe the colonists in their first hard years. And they kept on feeding frontier folk who kept on moving westward. In our history as a nation, white-tailed

Virginia deer have played a most important part.

They still play a part in the lives of many of us wherever they are numerous, whether we hunt them with gun or camera or just our eyes and ears. For most of the states now have good laws allowing hunting only at such seasons as will not reduce the deer faster than they can renew themselves. Because whitetails live so successfully in settled regions, states like New York and Pennsylvania, full of large towns and cities, now have many deer in their wooded portions. And many a man helps feed his family for a pleasant spell each winter with good deer meat.

It seems a shame that so many fine wild animals should annually be shot. But actually it must be done lest all the deer, bucks, does and fawns, die of slow starvation.

Most natural enemies of deer have disappeared from forests close to settled places. Human hunters have to take the place of panthers, bobcats, wolves, and bears. Without one check or the other, deer multiply too rapidly. Fifty does will bear some seventy-five fawns every year, and in two years the first fawns will be having more fawns of their own. With so many mouths to feed, the forest food supply is soon

the more
persistent
enemies

exhausted. All leaves and twigs and even bark are bitten from the brush and trees as high as the tallest deer can reach. Every new little plant is eaten up before it barely starts to grow. Winter comes. The weak and hungry deer die of the cold. Too feeble to fight, they cannot even run from the few wild enemies still in the wood. Death fills the forest and the snow is strewn with wretched carcasses.

This has happened wherever the hunters were kept out of the forests for too many years. It is a case not of eating your venison and having it too, but of killing some deer to save the rest. Too much protection only leads to suffering for all. Since we, for safety's sake, must rid the regions where we live of wolves and wildcats, we must manage the deer for their own good. Thus all of us, the deer included, really benefit as the hunter pursues his pleasure within the limits of wise laws.

Perhaps harder than the hunter on all wild

life is the man who cuts the woods in a wasteful way, but worst of all is he who, through plain carelessness, sets the forests afire. News of these fires sets us ablaze with indignation. Yet as far as deer are concerned, we can take a little comfort in this fact: after the axman has cut the evergreens, leafy forests may replace them. This new and different timber is a long time growing, but eventually it is better suited to the deer and most wild animals than the spruce and pine and hemlock forest was, though a mixture is best of all. The same thing happens where the fire has been, as berry bushes, birches, beeches, oaks, and other nut trees slowly grow. It takes a full lifetime for us, and the lifetimes of many deer, to see the scars so healed. But once they are, future animals and some of our descendants may enjoy the woodlands more.

Since whitetails are so widespread, we may almost say that wherever there's a leafy forest of at least one hundred acres, even though it is near a noisy town, there these sagacious deer are likely to be lurking. And if you like to lurk there too, and have a quiet way about you in the woods, sooner or later you may see them. Before this happens you may know that they are there by many signs. Where grass grows in some open glade you may see, in the morning, spaces where it lies quite flat, as though held down by something heavy for some time before you came along. Such depressions are the night beds of the deer. There they have rested, chewing their cuds in comfort, but wide awake and ready to steal into the underbrush, hiding there from real or fancied foe, from whatever side of

the glade they might have thought they heard him coming.

A day bed deep in the thicket, perhaps against some fallen tree, you are far less likely to discover. Wherever it is, the deer is almost sure to lie so that he can watch his back trail and spy you there in time to slip away in silence. On the other hand, a group of deer may spend long rainy spells deep in dense clumps of low branched evergreens which grow on knolls where least water will get in and least remain, and needle-covered ground is good to lie upon. Seek them in such snuggeries. Bed will be in a different place with every change of weather. For deer want the wind to warn them of their enemies, and they like to lie well sheltered from the rain.

By examining the brush you may at least find where your elusive friends have fed, the leaves and twigs being bitten off in places. On mossy ground you will discover many dents made by the feeders' feet. Had you the keen nose of a dog, these footprints would have taken your attention first, for each is flavored from the scent glands which deer have between their toes.

In early autumn look for deer tracks under oaks and beeches, for here they will come to fatten on their favorite fruit, acorns and nuts, before winter's cold descends upon them. They never touch the wormy ones, knowing at a whiff which ones are bad. Later in the fall, when heavy frosts come every night and are slow to melt each morning, go early and watch by the edges of swamps and ponds where the warmth of the water has kept the nearby plants from freezing. Here is where the deer will come for breakfast.

The colder the weather grows, the more they will seek the swampy or lower land where thick clumped knolls give shelter, and from which they can bolt in the bat of an eye into the surrounding tangle if you surprise them in their beds. Perhaps as winter closes in you will find one of their yards, a place where the snow is trampled by the feet of a large group of deer which have gathered for the colder months. From it, much used paths will lead through the

snow to places where twigs and buds and moss and other winter fare is to be found. On balmy days when a thaw sets in, they will take siestas up the southern slopes of partly wooded hills, where they can watch below while basking in the midday sun.

Of course, reading tales told by the tracks of all woodland animals is much easier in the snow, if it is not too deep, but in summer, too, you will find the paths or runways of the deer. They have favorite places where they often go, thus making well trod trails upon the forest floor. Here, wherever there is mud, you will see the surest sign of all, the seal of their sharply pointed cloven hoofs.

Now you may guess pretty well whom you are following. A doe's tracks, some two and three-fourths inches long, will point straight ahead or tend to toe in just a trifle. Most of the time the hind feet step nearly in the forefeet tracks. A buck's are bigger by a quarter inch or so, and probably will point out at least a little. They may have blunter points too, from pawing the ground and a tendency to drag their toes, especially in the autumn. This makes scuff

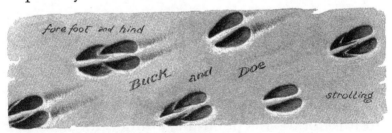

fore foot and hind

Buck and Doe

strolling

marks before their footprints. Only when they gallop, covering ten to twenty feet at a bound, or when they walk in snow will they make an imprint with their little upper, hinder hoofs. Of course if the doe is a big one or the buck is small, your guesses may be quite erroneous.

Following the trail is fun for a while, but you will hardly ever come upon the deer by doing so. With their wondrous ears and noses they already know you are there. They have not run away. More probably they have stepped a little off the path, and through some leafy screen are looking at you as you go along. It is fun to feel that this is so, but far more fun to look at them instead. You will not succeed by trying to peek through brush as they do, for you will have to move to do so and that will send them scooting. Though somewhat nearsighted and probably color blind, they notice any motion instantly. The more you move about, especially if the woods are dry and noisy, the less likely you will be to see any deer.

The better way is far easier. In plain sight of the path, as it crosses a clearing, sit down where you can ease your back against a tree. If possible, have the sun behind you, the "spotlight" on the scene you watch, yourself in shadows. Be sure the wind blows from the path to you, so that you will not be scented. And make no sound. Their ears and noses are far keener than their eyes.

Sit very still and you stand a good chance of not being noticed, though if you are, your utter stillness will excite more curiosity than fear. They may snort and freeze, but if you yourself stay frozen, they will be the first to tire of the game. It may take quite a while, but any shape that just won't wiggle isn't worthy of too much worry, they appear to think.

On the contrary, for all your care to sit down-wind, they may already have been following you, sniffing at your footprints. If in spite of this they are still upon the path, they are in no panic

and you will get your look. You will not be
pleased if, instead of deer, some of the nearest
farmer's pigs or sheep at last come down the
trail! It takes experience sometimes to tell a
whitetail's tracks from theirs.

But if you find a real deer path that leads to a
favorite drinking place at some pond or stream,
sit on the opposite bank of an evening. Presently
you may hear the soft swish of thick shrubbery
as the thirsty deer push gently through, for they
will not approach the water in an unprotected
place. Before it grows too dark you very well
may see a fade-in of their fine wild faces, ears
moving endlessly, seeking any slightest sound
which may mean danger. For several moments
they will wait, watching, listening. Finally, one
will drink and then the other, but never both
together. If there are more than two, one at least
will act as sentry for the others. As dusk deep-
ens, thirsts satisfied, they fade out, merging
subtly with the shadows.

Let us hope the punkies and mosquitoes do not find you just as the deer appear, for you must not even move an ear. Late afternoon and early morning, when whitetails are most active, are the very hours when insects seek most avidly to suck the patient watcher's blood. But such unwelcome company may come upon the deer themselves even in the heat of the day, and drive them to the water to soak in temporary refuge from their tiny but intolerable tormentors.

If succulent water plants, especially yellow water lilies, are growing there, a feast of these is added to the pleasure of relief from heat and

insect pests. The deer duck their heads below the water to pluck entire plants, eating stems, leaves, and flowers, and even swim to get them where they cannot stand upon the bottom. Should you come upon them there, instead of running, an experienced buck may sink till only his nose is out, perhaps hoping you will mistake his antlers for dead branches in the water. The times this clever trick succeeds may far outnumber times when it fails, for the latter are the only times we know about.

Whitetails are inclined to try craft first, and run only as the last resort. From the moment they are born with a coat of perfect camouflage, they learn to lie low and let an enemy pass. If they must move, and think they have not been seen, they will sneak under an object whenever possible, or even through a barbed wire fence, rather than leap over it and make themselves conspicuous. They probably save their lives many more times by such methods than by crashing noisily away. But if in headlong flight a bit of hurdling becomes necessary, they can sail over seven foot obstacles with all celerity.

A doe is more inclined to trust to tricks than is a buck. She will lie till the last minute, legs gathered under and ready to go, but hoping your course will miss her as you wander in the woods. And by the laws of chance, it is very likely to. Of course, if it doesn't miss, she will, with whistling snort and tail held high, burst from her bed like a jack-in-the-box and be gone with all speed, presumably to get as far away as possible, to reach Peru or Patagonia perhaps. But in one or two hundred yards she will stop and stand still, listening a long time. If it seems no enemy is following, she will back-track on her trail a little way, still watchful, then steal into the nearest cozy thicket, lie down and go on with the pleasant work of chewing cuds.

Even though disturbed repeatedly, whitetails will continue to stay in the special neck of the woods which they consider home. It may be a mere matter of one square mile, or even less, but they love it and won't leave it even when it is full of hunters. Half a dozen men or more may "beat" the woods, walking noisily in a wide flung line, to scare the deer down runways where other hunters wait. But the crafty creatures, like as not, will still be on their home grounds when the men have passed, having sneaked between the beaters and lain down behind them.

In some states sanctuaries are set aside, sections of wilderness watched by wardens, where deer are safe even in the hunting season. There they increase in peace and comfort, and from there spread into the surrounding countryside. But well they know the difference between the protected and unprotected places, many flocking back to the security of their fawnhood home until the gunning is all over for the year.

Deer seem to know when the hunting season

opens and when it ends. Though hunters have
been about all summer, stalking other things,
the deer have not felt too disturbed. Almost any
morning, early, and often in the evening, we see
them near our home on the forest's edge. The
deer season opens, and now we see no living deer,
only the carcasses of the unwise, unlucky few,
borne home by the hunters. For a few weeks the
countryside seems full of men with guns. But
finally the season ends. And then, the very next
morning, there are deer browsing peacefully
quite near the house. How do they know the
siege is over?

Animals often seem to sense things we can
only learn by looking at our books and calendars.
But though so very bright, the whitetails have
their failings. Sooner or later their very love of
home may bring about disaster. Refusing to
leave "for parts unknown," at least until the
shooting stops, they run repeated risks of being
killed by staying close to home. A hunter can

study the stamping grounds of a certain group of deer just as you can, and eventually he will be watching as they walk along a favorite trail.

The love of salt may make for trouble too. Needing it, as do all ruminants, for good health's sake, deer will go many miles to lick a certain spot of soil which has some salt or other minerals in it. A hunter can watch at such a place. Or, knowing no salt-lick, he can create one by putting salt all over an old stump, and wait for the deer which are sure to smell it from afar.

One fact, however, may save many a buck from such an ambush. They do most of their salt eating in the spring and summer while their antlers grow. In the fall they are so full of such important affairs concerning does and rivals that the salt lure is likely to go unnoticed till the hunting season is over.

If a deer eating in the open is alone, a man can sometimes sneak upwind right toward it, by moving only when its head is down. Always before it looks up it will wiggle its tail. This unconscious nervous habit gives the man his cue to stand and freeze. Since to shortsighted whitetail eyes unmoving objects are just so much landscape, the hunter can get close enough for a shot before the game observes him, unless he accidentally makes some noise in stalking.

If a hunter has followed a buck all day, forever finding himself no nearer the quarry, he can figure that the animal is almost as tired as he is. But by then it has had so many hours of his trailing that, if he suddenly sits down at the near edge of a clearing the deer has crossed, in more cases than not it will wonder what is keeping him and actually come back to see! Curiosity is sometimes fatal, though no intelligent creature can learn anything without it.

In the fall a buck may be so set on finding mates and rivals that any other ideas are quite crowded from his mind. Fear and caution have deserted him, and he will stand listening as you approach, waiting to see if you are a doe or a buck to battle. He may prove dangerous to an unarmed person then. In some places a man need only clash a pair of old cast antlers together, rattle them, pause, clash them again, and so on, to call deer of both sexes to him. They gather as we do, to witness some excitement; they think two unseen bucks are fighting.

So much for the weaknesses of adult deer. What are the failings of the fawns? Fawns are frisky children. In spite of strong instincts to freeze or hide for safety's sake, which all deer have, playful impulses and innocent friendliness make them break the rules sometimes. Then a mother must use discipline; not like the she-bear which can cuff her cubs and send them sprawling, but gently though firmly.

The first weeks in the life of a whitetail fawn are properly spent entirely in hiding. For almost a month it must stay concealed, then it begins to go about with its mother more and more. But, being a baby, it wants to be with her from the start, and may try to follow when she goes to eat and drink. Or it may merely want to romp when safety demands that it be very still. Then mother may press it gently to the ground with her nose or forefoot which usually is enough to make it mind.

Her plan is to suckle it every now and then, but not to stay beside it till it is old enough to run from dogs or wolves or wildcats, and too big to interest a fox or eagle. At birth a big one will not weigh four full pounds, having a body the size of a cat though with much longer legs. It is very nearly minus any odor now, so enemies are not likely to discover it unless it moves about. For when quiet, it is only a mound or an old prone log with sunlight spotted on it through the leafy trees.

Mother stays near enough to hear its squeaky voice if it calls, though this it is not supposed to do unless some danger threatens it all unknown to her, which rarely will occur, so alert is she concerning everything about her baby. By being near but not too near, her movements, tracks, and adult scent will take an enemy's attention so that she can fight it, if that's feasible, or lead it far away. A dog has been known to jump right over a crouching fawn he neither saw nor scented, while dashing at the mother, after which he went bawling off through the woods in hot but useless pursuit as she led him far

away.

A young doe will have one fawn about the month of her second birthday, but generally twins each year thereafter, sometimes triplets. She hides them all in separate spots and has a big task taking care of such a family. Among other hazards it may happen that in moving her fawn or fawns she is confronted by a poisonous snake, perhaps a cottonmouth or rattler, which can deal death to her children in the smallest fraction of a second.

Instantly she bounds in air and comes down stiff-legged with all four feet together, full on the snake, plunging eight spear-pointed toes into it with all the weight of her body. She lands as near its head as possible, for then its fangs striking upward will hit only horny hoofs. But there's always the risk that the swinging head will lash around and stab deadly venom into one of her legs. Better this than let it bite her baby, is her motto. And when no other plan will

work, like other mothers of the wild, she will fight far bigger foes than snakes to save her little ones.

For all her courage, cunning, and concern, she sometimes loses fawns, of course. Predators like pumas, bobcats, wolves, and such, do take a toll of newborn young each year. They are not to be condemned for this. They know nothing of closed or open seasons, but hunt to live the year around, and feed young families of their own. Nature has equipped these animals to live on meat alone, and favors them as much as any others. It was the everlasting efforts of such as they to eat the ancestors of deer and antelope which, through the ages, brought about the latter's present fleetness and keen watchfulness and craft. Dullards didn't do so well, and died.

It's all a part of the mighty scheme of life, which is an endless struggle to survive, won only by the strongest, swiftest, or the most intelligent. It takes strength and speed and wits to catch a deer, and the same good qualities to escape time after time to raise more young, who will in turn succeed or fail according to their aptitudes.

Sometimes a doe does not return to her hiding fawn. All her care won't always save her from

some enemy. Then the little one may cry in lonely hunger, and this is bad because enemy ears can hear it, though she cannot. At length it takes to wandering and may be lucky enough to find another doe which will adopt and feed it, and care for it with her own.

All any fawn should follow is the big white flash of its mother's or its foster mother's tail. White is the color that carries farther than all others, and the monochrome nearsighted little one can see it even though the rest of the brownish parent is all blurred and lost to view among the shadows of the forest. When she runs she holds it high, and waggles it from side to side as the signal "Follow me." She leads the enemy away by this device as well. But having no experience in the world, the lonesome fawn may elect to follow a passing horse, though a man is on its back, or even you as you walk in the woodland. Such orphans have been raised by farmers' goats, or on cow's milk from a baby's bottle.

For its first year such a creature makes a charming pet, and may for many years thereafter. But it is never really tame, just not timid, and once full grown is never truly safe for constant company. In all the ancient history behind it, there have been few persons whom any deer could look upon as anything but an enemy. It may not happen with your pet, but then again it's always possible that sooner or later, in spite of all your friendliness, the old deep-rooted feelings suddenly will fill its heart. Then it will forget all else and strike you down, bruising and slashing with its strong sharp hoofs.

Pet does have cut up people very seriously, and "tame" bucks have sometimes killed their keepers. A buck in the mating season, with brand new antlers on his head, is indeed quite likely to go berserk and hurt somebody or something very badly. There was a case of a pet buck which turned on a billygoat with which it had been raised. The goat met the attack in good goat style but, being more of a butter than a fencer like the deer, soon lost his life. As he made a charge head on, the buck sidestepped and caught him in the flank. He was tossed high in air and came down dead, a mass of broken ribs and punctures.

Having lost all fear of humans, a pet buck may be much more dangerous than a wild one. But even wild ones, half crazy with the will to fight all real or imaginary rivals for about two months each fall, will come from the woods at times to attack a man, or a team of horses, or even an automobile! Autos can feel no pain, but they can be badly bent and scratched and possibly punctured in encounters of this kind. And the worst of it is, in some parts of our land the law says that anyone who kills a deer in any manner whatsoever, unless he has a hunting license, must pay a fine. Add this to the damage the deer did to your car, and to yourself in the crash, and you will feel that though he died a-doing it, he got the best of you for all that.

Though a good many deer are killed crossing highways, the cases of bucks actually attacking cars can hardly be called common. For the most part bucks fight bucks. Some bouts begin in mid-October, but the tournament is really on full tilt around the middle of November. As the season draws near, two bucks, which may have been good chums all summer, watching for each

other's safety at the drinking place, pulling
pesky wood-ticks from each other's fur, sleeping
side by side, will spar with each other, rather
playfully at first. They may, while browsing, attack each other as if in fun, and quit in a moment after a mere rattle and push with antler to
antler. Almost any helpless, innocent bush may
have to take some sudden, savage slashes. It
looks like play or practice at most, but the physi-
cal condition and state of mind of the bucks is
changing steadily.

Day by day their necks swell, till fully half
again their usual size. Finally comes a day when,
having met a doe perhaps, they really have a

serious set-to. Depending on how well they are matched, the struggle will be brief or hours long. One may issue a challenge with a ratchety blaat. He paws the ground. Both shake their heads, well aware of their weapons. Like goats or rams they come together with a clash. Unlike these, they do not break away and clash again repeatedly, but stay in close, pushing each other back and forth with mouths open, fencing and guarding and watching for a chance to jab.

Ears may be slit or pierced, but on the whole so good are their antlers for defense that as long as each stands his ground he is fairly safe from serious injury. When at last one wearies of the fight and turns to flee, if he isn't quick about it, he may be badly hurt, possibly killed. If he makes a good clean getaway, he's not likely to be followed very far. The victor will turn back to claim his well-won mate. He probably will have to fight still other bucks to keep her, but is willing to and eager.

His vanquished chum, after a rest, will try again, possibly with an opponent easier to overcome. Whether there's a doe in the offing or not, any buck will duel with any other anywhere near its equal. Young spikehorns and old gray grandpas will clear out of the woods where a prime buck with eight or ten points or more is ranting about and spoiling for a fight. The one will live to grow a better set of antlers before he takes up any challenge; the other has had his years of glory, and grows ever poorer crowns each year.

You cannot tell a buck's age with any certainty, however, by his size or the number of points his antlers bear. Much depends on how well he is and how well he has lived. He will have just two little bumps or buttons in the first summer and fall of his life. Then, ordinarily in his second summer, he will grow his two short spikes which he sheds in winter. By the third spring, his second birthday, he will be growing a pair of pointed beams bearing one branch each, giving him two points on either side. By his third birthday he will be wearing beams with two up-jutting branches each, or three points apiece, six in all, and so on, adding a pair of points every year. But some young bucks go for several seasons with only spikes, like lads who cannot get beyond first grade for quite a while. Others, just as young, may add more than one new pair of points each year, like chaps who skip some grades and get along more rapidly. Whitetails may have several dozen points, but this is freakish and may be due to injuries while in the velvet.

Once in a while two well-matched bucks of the same size and armed with nearly equal antlers both die in battle. It happens to various kinds of deer but probably most often to the whitetails. The single beams of their antlers, bearing many points, bend forward midway and slightly inward, being like two many-barbed hooks. Once they slip past each other, it may be harder than a Chinese puzzle pulling them apart.

The bucks are each the other's death trap then, much as both would gladly break away. The weaker one dies of thirst or hunger, to be dragged by the stronger as he tries to feed and get to water, only to perish too, at last. In the olden days before we killed so many predators, such a suicide pair would soon be out of their misery, slain by wolves or other enemies, a merciful, quick conclusion of their hopeless draw. Nowadays such unfortunates may be found by men in time to be sawed apart and sent on their respective ways rejoicing.

Besides battling for the does, whitetail bucks make muddy hollows by pawing up the ground and wetting it, then getting down and wallowing in it there. When they are utterly soiled and smelling as musky and strong as possible, they seem to feel that they are irresistible. Maybe it's a way of wearing warpaint to scare their rivals and impress the does they hope to fascinate. No one can figure out just why a buck in such a state should have an ounce of charm. Yet the females find him not the least offensive.

A buck may mate with one doe or two or three, but never more. His feelings are for a family rather than a harem. Unlike the wapiti buck, he doesn't desire to be the boss of a whole big herd of does. The excitement of the season soon subsides, and whatever does run with him are rejoined by their fawns, a mixed group of half a dozen deer or so thus forming. These fawns, now weaned a month or so, are already acting more like adults in their new gray-brown winter coats. All feed and fatten on acorns and other good fall fare, for winter surely is on the way.

As the weather comes on ever snowier, this family group will "yard up" with others like it, making a mingled herd of bucks and does of all

sizes and ages. They choose a place for the yard where browse will be close by and sufficient to last a long time, preferably till spring. As the snows pile up, the paths to their food grow deeper and deeper, till sometimes a deer can run along in one and not be visible from another.

Knowing all the paths by heart may save a deer's life now and then, but beasts of prey are liable to spend the winter near the yard since their food supply is so conveniently collected in a cold storage pantry. So winter is a triply dangerous time for the deer, what with severe cold, scantier food, more persistent enemies plus poorer chances of escape. A deer in deep snow where there is no path cannot travel as fast or well as a big-pawed panther, nor as well as wolves and coyotes which can do a kind of stomach-skiing over soft snow, and run rapidly over crust that won't support a deer.

Something which doesn't help them any is the universal loss of antlers which takes place in January. Old bucks in good condition may shed them in December, but ailing bucks and young spikehorns may carry theirs till March. But for every deer's defense against all animal enemies, the good sharp-edged cloven hoofs remain the ever ready and reliable.

Spring comes at last, and with the melting of the snow much needed tender greens are soon found everywhere. The herd breaks up, grown bucks going off in twos and threes, the does in little bands with their fawns of the spring before, now almost one year old. These nearly yearling youngsters are quite on their own by May, for each adult doe goes off by herself to have her new spring family. So the summer comes and goes. While does nurse their off-spring, bucks nurse offshoots of bone upon their heads till fall, and another time of mating and dueling is at hand.

In captivity whitetails have lived for twenty-five years, but in the wilderness, what with accidents in dashing through thick woods and numerous enemies, they are lucky if their lives last half that long. You now must have a pretty good idea of how a whitetail's life is lived. The lives of other deer are different, but somewhat similar. I shall not need to tell of them in quite so much detail.

M U L E   D E E R

YOU have heard the expression, "I can't believe my ears." This is one of the mule deer's very worst worries. Though their ears are enormous and probably catch more sound than ears of other deer, it's possible they may catch too much sometimes. A band of them are so shocked by some sudden sound, that instead of instantly dashing for cover, they all jump high in the air, facing every which way, then mill round and round each other for pre-

cious moments before being able to decide which
way to run. Their noses and eyes are evidently
just as keen as whitetails' but sometimes they
seem more confused than aided by their ears. So

strong are impressions received by the ears that those taken in by nose and eyes are often over-looked entirely. Seeing a second source of danger is not believing it, if they have heard some other danger first. Scared by some unseen enemy in the brush, they will ignore you as they flee, though you may be moving and in plain sight. If really scared, they seem able to manage only one fright at a time.

On the other hand, if they see or smell a prowler, or hear his steps gradually following their trail, they will sneak from their beds, skulk through the cover, and circle in behind him to lie down again in peace, about as cleverly as whitetails do. The big difference is that in sudden trouble they are soon scared out of their wits, whereas whitetails usually are not. In the heat of summer, deer sometimes sleep while standing. A drowsy buck will stand under some low tree where he can fend off flies by bobbing his head through leafy branches. Each time he

does this there is such a rattle of bone on boughs about his ears that he cannot hear a stalking enemy. Predators, by moving only when he shakes his head, creep toward him all too easily. There is sure to come a day when he will sleep this way just once too often.

But mostly mule deer do their sleeping lying down. It isn't likely you will ever see a sign "Mule Deer Hotel." Yet there are places in the western wilderness which are called just that, and rightly so, by woodsmen. Favorite hillsides, well sheltered from the wind and where the sun shines long each day, are sometimes found completely pitted by the beds of deer. For though the bucks make no muddy wallows in the autumn mating time, many mule deer make most ambitious beds by hollowing out the hillside with their hoofs.

Through nearly constant use between the early morning and late evening dining hours, these resting spots grow ever deeper and cozier, their bottoms becoming an ever softer, finer dust. Some beds are single, some big enough for two. Can you see the mule deer resting in their own hotel, as contented as a herd of cud-chewing cows, except that their oversized ears move unceasingly, seeking any ominous sound even as their owners sleep?

Mule deer occur in much of the country between northern Alberta in Canada and San Luis Potosi in Mexico, and from the eastern edge of the western plains clear into California. In all this area there are many kinds of climate, which have given rise to various types of mule deer. But whatever the conditions, hot, cold, dry, or humid, they tend as a rule to keep to the rough and rugged places, hilly or mountainous country broken by ravines and gorges, caring little for vast stretches of uninterrupted timber nor yet for open plains.

Even when they do wander out on the open countryside, they tend to range not too far from the mountains or rocky upjuttings in the desert. It is very unwise for mule deer to stray upon the plains, for though they differ in different parts of their range, all are alike as to gait, and this is most unsuited to safe living on the level. It is fit only for life in a lumpy land and is designed to carry the deer in jumps from lump to lump, uphill or down, while pursuers scramble in amongst the lumps and soon give up.

Though mule deer walk or trot like white-tails, in urgent haste they do not gallop, but leave the ground and land with all four feet to-gether in long stiff-legged leaps. From rock to rock this is ideal. But as a substitute for gallop-ing in the open it is fast for a little way but very tiring. Unless the jumping deer can reach their hills and gullies quickly, they are easily run

down by dogs, wolves, coyotes, or men on horse-back with lassos.

Once let them gain the rocky hills however, and they are in their element. Nothing can catch them there. Bounding from rock to rock and up and up and over gullies far too wide for enemies to follow, they fairly float up hillsides like the shadows of fast moving clouds, and seem to go as lightly.

In the dry southwest and Mexico, they often must dash for their lives through thorn infested brush and cactus, though they could go around most clumps of vegetation if they weren't in such a dither. Most of them carry many spines deeply imbedded in their flesh. But deer, though delicate in some ways, are very tough in others, often recovering from wounds much worse than those made by the cactus spines. These desert mule deer depend entirely on dew and deft bites taken between the spines of cactus plants for all the water they obtain through much of the year.

In the cooler, better watered parts of their range, the bucks having spent the summer in the high, sunny, flyless regions close to timberline, go down to lower levels where the does have been raising fawns. After the mating season with its defeats and triumphs, mixed bands descend still farther into milder, better sheltered sections of the hills. Here the snow is not too deep to dig for fallen leaves, lichens, mosses and so on, and brush buds and the like are still accessible.

Unlike the whitetails, mule deer will go at least a hundred miles to find good winter ranges if they must. Here several hundred will get through the harder months, following faithfully the leadership of some old doe, which doubtless is the mother, grandma, and great grandmamma of so many of them. In her, whose wisdom has protected numerous helpless fawns, all place their trust.

As with the whitetails, these deer are biggest in the cooler country. Standing as high as whitetails, they are heavier and more stocky. A giant buck would weigh four hundred and fifty pounds or a little more, but he'd be very rare. Big ones weigh three hundred pounds, but the average is about two hundred. The antlers are not on the beam-with-points plan, but generally grow right up and branch and then branch again. With a snag at the base of each antler, they thus have five points to the side, ten points in all. But some may go on branching more and more, the head of one deer on record having eighteen points on one side and nineteen on the other.

It seems unnecessary to say that mule deer are so named because of their mighty ears. But some say the style of the tail is included, for this is thin and nearly cylindrical and ends in a black tip slightly wider. The hair on this tip is shed but once a year, though all the rest is changed in fall and spring, giving mule deer a red-brown summer coat and a blue-brown one for winter, a good deal grayer than the whitetail's. But instead of being raised when the mule deer flees from danger, the tail is swung back and forth across the rump like a black pendulum on a white clock, thus telling fawns and friends it's high time to be leaving.

Blacktail

Besides the snowy rump, a mule deer has white on its face, belly, inside the legs, and a patch on its throat. There is a black bar under the chin and a big dark patch upon the forehead. The spotted fawns are the color of yellow clay with white daisies growing in it. So much for mule deer. They have close relatives living in the mountains on the Pacific coast from Alaska to California. These deer are known as black-tails because that color covers the entire tail on the upper side, though it is white below. They are smaller, and they like thick woodland better, but get over the ground in the very same jumping, bounding, mule deer way.

W A P I T I

THROUGH no fault of their own, the
wapiti have been called elk by millions
of Americans ever since the pioneers so
misnamed them. Moose are the real American
elk whose Old World kin are the European elk,
as you can see in the illustration farther on. So let
us call our own big stags wapiti, a real American
name to which they have a perfect right, having

received it from the Shawnee Indians long before the coming of the white man. It means "pale deer" and refers to the winter coat which bleaches slowly till quite light by spring.

Like the moose, they too have relatives across the seas, widespread from Morocco through much of Asia, Europe, and the British Isles. "The stag at eve" who had "drunk his fill" in Scott's poem was our own big stag's close cousin. All members of this group of deer are large, whether natives of cold Siberia or the tropics, but the wapiti themselves are the largest deer in the world save for the moose. Stags average five feet high at the shoulders, weighing seven hundred pounds, but some are so tall as to weigh a thousand. Even the fawns weigh thirty pounds the day they are born.

Wapiti, first found in Virginia in 1650, long after Raleigh wrote about the whitetails, were met in eastern Canada in 1535. At that time these deer, "as big as horses," ranged almost all the future country of the United States, from Canada to Mexico, from Atlantic to Pacific. And from Atlantic to Pacific, following the very trails the great deer made, pioneers fed upon them as they did on whitetails. Without them—food ready made for people pushing through the wilderness—our country would have grown very much more slowly.

Less wily than the smaller whitetails and less adaptable, these great deer steadily gave ground before the westward push of settlers, until today nearly all our wapiti will be found in western national parks where Uncle Sam gives them year round protection. Not browsers, but grazers just as much as cows and sheep and horses, they were being driven ever higher into the hills and mountains to make room for ranchmen's livestock. In the west it was their habit to seek high land in summertime, and come down in autumn to fertile, far more level lands, where forage could be found all winter.

But more and more, as men moved in, the great grass-eating deer found their way blocked by bullets and barbed wire, or if not these, the grass already eaten or cut and carried off to stacks and guarded by the ranchers' guns. Sudden death or slow starvation would have been the fate of all these last survivors had not good citizens seen to it then that some few places were set aside as their very own, inviolate.

Now, wintering in the parks and rarely reaching ranchland lower down, they are fed by forest rangers with good hay, if forage in the mountains grows scarce. As for cold, like the warm-robed bison, bighorn sheep, and mule deer, they never mind sub-zero weather. They can lie for hours in a pawed-out bed of snow, hardly melting a flake of it, so snug is their winter coat, so able to keep their own warmth in while shutting out the cold. They suffer only if day after day, in digging down through the deep snow, they find no food to keep the fires of life burning brightly in their bodies.

But though winter is long, spring comes at last, and the herds follow the melting snow up higher every day, clear to the timberline, feasting on flowers and tender greens. Journeying upward, they stick together, feeding by day and sleeping at night with the stags outermost, the hinds and half-grown fawns inside the ring. Now wolves and panthers had best beware. Once on the heights however, every animal goes off alone, the hinds to have their spotted fawns each by herself, the stags to sprout and cultivate new antlers.

Wondrous these antlers are, fully five feet long on the bigger stags, two beautiful branching beams springing backward, and a set of four big spikes before the face like the prongs of some terrible kind of giant cow-catcher. And in a way of speaking they do catch the cows, as female wapiti are often called, fighting for them with these great weapons.

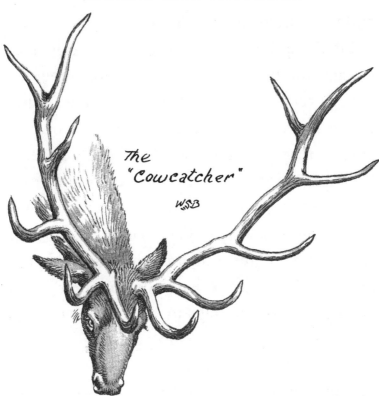

The "Cowcatcher"

WSB

But before the autumn tournaments come months of peace and pleasure in the mountains. Females and fawns, after the latter's first few days, join one another and, with the yearlings, form happy herds, having few worries and able to cope with all comers. A bear goes by and isn't

fool enough to bother them. If he thinks he has
a chance to catch a fawn off by itself, he soon has
a host of furious females taking all the tuck out
of him. For the fawn's mother summons help
with a loud cry while getting in some fast work

with her five-inch, sharp-edged, heavy hoofs.

Meantime the stags, both old and young, gather in bands of their own, all friendly in their velvet days. They have climbed even higher than the hinds, where banks of snow persist all summer. Here no flies torment, and cold streams "cool their fevered brows," hot with antlers growing heavier day by day. They sometimes have impromptu dances out of sheer exuberance in the summertime, a band suddenly running in a circle, noses near the ground, with every so often a jump of joy as they turn and churn for several minutes at a time.

Finally, with September, comes the time of changing costumes from summer's rusty brown to coats of thick blue-gray. Snowstorms start the stags down early from the heights, and all their summer harmony is over. Now it is everyone for himself, and not "the devil take the hindmost," but every devil takes the most hinds he can—for his harem. A grand champion may manage to maintain a band of twenty females for himself alone, but in doing so must fight all who challenge his supremacy.

Being so big and therefore not secretive, the wapiti are noisy in their duels. The voice of a full-grown stag makes mighty music on the autumn air. Day and night they sing out the call and battle one another. It isn't easy to describe the call. Some speak of it as a bugle, some as a whistle, and some suggest blowing hard across the mouth of a half-pint bottle to get an inkling of the tone. This and the whistle idea belong together, for no shrill noise is meant by the word, but more the vibrant and stentorian sound of a steamboat siren. Truth is, some of the challenge is steamboat whistly and some silver bugly.

The big stag starts with a deep throaty roar which rises to clear strong bugling only to shatter itself in a whistling scream, which comes shivering back into the animal's throat and disappears in two or three fierce grunts. When he's through, you have heard something. But you'll hear more, for he gets answers right away from almost any of the old boys within the wide range of a mile. By the vigor of his notes other stags can gauge the probable powers of the challenger.

Soon one who deems himself a logical contender comes snorting up, and the battle is on. Growling and grinding their teeth with noses close to forefeet, they move around each other, watching for a chance to hit where it will hurt. Suddenly one sees an opening, but as he smashes in, a turn of the head brings the other one's antlers into line and neither one is injured. They back off as the racket of their collision echoes through the hills. Again, with open mouths, they crash together, head to head, and push and strain, scattering stones and tearing up the turf.

Thus it goes until one knows in his heart that the other eventually will win. Watching his chance, he suddenly turns and runs for it, getting neither gored nor even nicked if he is lucky.

Tough hide and hair on their necks and shoulders help while the fight continues, but once one turns his unprotected flank or rear, he has to use all speed to escape. He's likely to go off at a gallop, but soon breaks into a much preferred trot, with which he gets over the ground at three and a third minutes to the mile.

The snow unrolls its deep white blanket farther down the mountains every day and soon is burying the battlefield. All feuds forgotten, the rivalry and mating over, old stags roam the slopes rounding up the stragglers for the fall return to lower sheltered valleys. The wapiti herds descend headed by a hind, a wise old grandmamma. The old stag may boss his little band, because he's bigger and better armed in autumn. He rules in a way, but he's not the leader. He can fight his way out of trouble, but the old hind is far better at avoiding it. So in the shifting to new territory, even he follows her, his customary place being in the rear, prodding on the laggards.

So once again, all fattened from the summer foraging, they yard up for a winter as the wards of Uncle Sam.

NEW WORLD

OLD WORLD

MOOSE

IF we could call together representatives of
every kind of deer in order to select their
chief mogul, we should doubtless choose
the bull moose for that honor. For though he is
positively homely, he's as intelligent as most,
and also is the tallest and heaviest, carrying the
most mightily impressive antlers of them all.
This applies as well, of course, to his Old World
kin, the European elk.

The average bull moose stands six feet high at the shoulders, weighs almost half a ton, and his antlers spread some fifty-seven inches from side to side. But in Alaska, where bull moose are bull moose indeed, individuals exist which are eight feet high, the height of the average circus elephant. Their antlers alone weigh sixty pounds and are six and a half feet wide or there-

abouts, a record set being fully seven. It takes a powerful animal to tote such ornaments around. Wearing the crown of Chief Mogul is a heavy responsibility.

The weight of the antlers is not the reason why his neck is short, but it seems fortunate that this is so. The longer the neck the harder to hold up a head so burdened. But of course the neck is short whether he has his antlers on or not, and so is the cow's neck and her calves'. Their necks are so short and their legs so long that they have to get down on their knees to eat any grass of ordinary length. For stuff that stands a little higher, they will place their forefeet wide apart

and spread to it like giraffes. Usually, as far as grasses go, they content themselves with nibbling daintily at the tops of the taller kinds, curling their clumsy-looking, overhanging upper lips about a wisp as deftly as an elephant employs its trunk.

But buds and tender leaves and twigs are much more moosely fare. The word "moose" is from an Indian name and signifies "twig eater." In winter they are very hard on moosewood (striped maple), willow, poplar, birch, cherry, alder, elder, mountain ash, and dogwood, and branch ends of balsam, cedar, and so on. After browsing as high as they can reach on all fours, they rear on their hind legs and reach still higher twigs. Small trees bend beneath their weight, and straddling these at ease, they eat off every twig and skin the bark from the upturned side of the trunk. About all they leave to such slim trees is a slender chance for their recovery. It takes at least thirty-five pounds of forage to feed

each moose each day, so that everything about a winter yard is pretty thoroughly mauled by spring or earlier. Then they must drift to some other spot where no moose has been for a long time and vegetation has renewed itself.

Their winter yards, unlike those of elk and mule deer, in the Yellowstone at least, are likely to be higher than the summer feeding grounds. They seek the sources of streams where ever-flowing springs prevent surrounding swamps from freezing very much, and go back to the lower places about the end of April. Before long they find, along stream sides and near the shores of ponds and lakes, perhaps their chief of feasting pleasures, yellow water lilies.

As summer advances they spend more and more time culling these succulent plants from the bottom. Heat and insects forgotten, they soak in the water and feed at will. A moose may stand in the shallows and duck his head to cut the lilies close to the roots, raising up with a dripping mouthful to chew. Or he can go out over his head and submerge completely for as much as a minute and a half, coming up for a breather and sinking again. There has been recorded more than one bad moment, disconcerting for both man and moose, when one suddenly has risen to the surface almost under a canoe.

Just how moose munch lilies under water no one knows, but they surely have some way of using their oversized lips so that water doesn't get mixed or swallowed with the food. Neither

can anyone be sure, but it's probable that the long, flappy ears are folded back along the neck to keep air in and water out. Besides this submarine style of meal, they consume vast quantities of other things in the summer: willow as usual, plus wild raspberry, honeysuckle, grass, weeds, ferns, and mushrooms.

But ever and again they return to their beloved lilies. As we've already seen, moose are excellent swimmers, a big bull with half a hundred pounds of bone atop his head being as able in the water as any crownless cow. Some woodsmen, seeing his ability, have thought they had the explanation of the "bell" which hangs beneath his throat. This wattle-like dependent piece of skin and hair is supposed to be inflated by the moose, somewhat like waterwings, to buoy up his heavy head in swimming.

Actually the bell's use, if any, is unknown. It may be the shriveled remnant of an organ once useful in the distant past to ancestors of moose;

but because of getting snagged on jagged branches and so forth, it is only a cause of difficulty now, like our tonsils, without which we live very well but which can give us trouble on occasion. Bulls have bells almost exclusively, but once in a while a cow does too. In fact, the biggest moose bell ever known, over a yard in length, was found on a female.

One wonders if in the mating season the rival bulls considered her more or less charming than the other cows because of this jabot, this far from dainty dewlap that dangled from her throat. Perhaps they never even noticed it at all. Their ideas of what makes a creature charming are very different from our own. This is the time of pungent perfume and no deer makes as odoriferous a mud wallow as the moose. Of course it is in this season that they are most dangerous to enemies and each other. With minds dull to all else but finding mates and fighting rivals, two bulls some evening hear the rising, falling moan of a lonesome cow, feeding in the lilies by some lake's shore. Each rushes toward the inviting sound, rattling his antlers on the brush and branches to let her know he is on his way, and grunting reassuringly lest she misconstrue his racket and take to her heels.

Once through the thickets, both bulls see the cow but also see each other, and with loathing. Their manes rise up in anger. One vents his wrath on the nearest bush, charging into it with vicious might, hooking it with antlers, tearing it to shreds and splinters with his flaying feet. "This is what I'll do to you!" his actions and his furious grunts imply. Meantime the other may be on his knees, not imploring mercy, but just as angrily grunting and gouging up the ground, ripping up roots and vines and tossing them all about with his antlers.

Then, shaking their shovel-shaped antlers, double duty shields and stabbers, slobbering froth with flapping lips and loudly champing their teeth, they fix each other with blood-reddened eyes. Pendulous nostrils open wide as they blow and paw the earth, approaching each other with temporary stiff-legged caution. Suddenly with snort and bellow their weapons clap together like the palms of two thunder-making giants playing pattycake!

It is amazing that antlers break so seldom under the terrific force of such collisions, each bull throwing his more than a thousand pounds at the other with all his insane power. It's still more amazing that there's anything left of the brains inside their skulls! It is true that in this season they act "punch drunk" much of the time. The wonder of it is that they ever get over it, but they do.

And when the wintry snow begins, the antlers are not used for shovels, as some people think. Their use is ended and they are soon shed. Some woodsmen say that the animals are right-or left-handed like ourselves. They say that moose habitually lie more on one side than the other. If this happens to be the left side, that antler will be smaller or more curving than the right, or vice versa. So they say, and indeed it is rare that antlers balance perfectly. Northwoodsmen in long winter evenings have time to tell tall stories. One told of giant trees growing very close together in a forest where dwelt a mighty moose with antlers fifteen feet across. When asked how a moose with such antlers managed to get about in such a place, he said that that was the moose's business.

And so it is, and a business he can manage very well, even when his antlers are in the velvet. Every summer, in a few of our northern states, in much of Canada, as far north as the timber grows, and in Alaska, moose develop their antlers with no more difficulty than other deer experience. Possibly they tend to move about in more open places while in the velvet. In regions where there is no open season, young bulls, which wander a good deal, have been known to spend long spells among tame cattle in the pasture.

Back in the wilder country, moose like to browse in the young green brush that grows on land burned over several years before. It is more open here, and among the blackened stumps and trunks of old scorched trees still standing they are pretty well disguised when stationary, being black with dark brown heads and grayish legs. Calves are a dull red-brown and spotless.

Moose have such long legs that in burned-over areas, where dead trees lie every which way,

they step over most of them with ease, where a
horse could not follow and a man must clamber.
Until the snow is six to eight feet deep, moose
do not consider yarding up, and get about quite
unimpeded. Cross country runners of the very
best are moose, moving at a swift but tireless
racehorse trot, their great splay feet, six inches
wide and seven long, taking them over every
kind of country, soft snow, solid ground, soggy
swamp, and through deep waters, up hill and
down dale with never a pause mile after mile,
the greatest steeplechasers in the world.

Even in these days of fast motor vehicles, it
must be fun indeed to ride behind one or a team
of these great deer trained to harness. Moose
raised by hand from calfhood have been so
trained many times and, save for about two
months each year, have proved splendid steeds.
But somehow, perhaps because they are too
powerful, none ever have been really put to
work the way the reindeer have, the Old World
deer whose cousins in America are the caribou.

REINDEER AND CARIBOU

MOST of us, when we think of reindeer, think of Santa Claus. Some few may think also of the faraway Laplanders who live with and on their reindeer herds, even migrating with them twice a year, using their cream-like milk, their meat, hides, bones and antlers for almost all necessities of life.

But few people think of the mighty herds of

caribou (American reindeer) ranging the wilds from Quebec to Alaska, and from the Canadian border clear to the Arctic Ocean. They are in Greenland too, and Siberia, Russia, and Scandinavia; members of their widespread brotherhood are found in all cold lands whose northern edges face the pole.

If we consider the word "reindeer" for a moment we may think it means a deer which is driven with reins. But the name was given these deer by their Lapland masters in whose language "reino" means pasture. These are their pasture deer which forever munch the moss on the treeless tundras, the open pastures of the north. Hitched to a sledge, these splendid steeds can make ten miles an hour and keep it up all day, but can sprint at twice that speed. Unhampered they can out-trot a horse with a stride as smooth as silk, and leave all natural enemies behind most of the time.

Even if the sledge lacks bells, the reindeer

themselves provide a sort of music when they move along. Within their legs, above the lesser toes of their very broad feet, are certain bones which click each time the hoofs are raised or pressed upon the ground. They keep up a clear clickety-click which continues whether they run or walk. The sound is made in somewhat the same way as when a person cracks his knuckles, but is louder. A large herd on the move creates a roar by the multitude of clickings all combined.

The hoofs of reindeer are still better than those of moose for getting over rocky or swampy ground, soft or crusted snow, or smoothest ice. Most deer are helpless on ice, but reindeer run right out on it, their extra sharp-edged feet skidding no more than skates do when they are forced sideways. Caribou have been known to rush onto the ice if wolves or hunters were behind them, and coast far out on their rumps. Then, as their enemies floundered after them, they would get to their feet and be off like the wind in another direction over the ice, making further pursuit quite useless.

They dash directly into water in the same reckless way, very different from the cautious approach by other deer to open spaces, wet or dry. They cannot swim as rapidly as moose or whitetails, but they cannot sink either. In the fall they have stored under the hide of their backs a layer of tallow fat, thin at the shoulders but thickening sometimes to six inches on the rump, a heat and energy storage scheme for the winter months. Maybe this helps to make them buoyant.

But they have a much more effective float at all seasons which holds them high in the water —their excellent overcoats. Outside their warm, oily underfur is a coarse thick coat of hairs, each of which is hollow and full of air. Thus if hungry Indians in canoes shoot into a herd of caribou crossing a lake or river, they never see their prize sink out of sight. The dead deer floats, buoyed up as by a billion bubbles, and is easily towed ashore. Non-sinkable suits are woven from this reindeer hair, and life belts are often stuffed with it. In their nearly constant roaming, caribou and reindeer never go around a body of water, but swim straight through it, picking up one of their well-worn trails on the other side.

The caribou can be divided into two main types—the woodland and the barren-ground caribou. The woodlander is the larger and longer-legged, standing four and a half feet at the shoulder and weighing from three to four hundred pounds. The barren-grounder is about three and a half feet high and weighs from two to three hundred pounds, about like the Old World reindeer. Both are colored in much the same pattern, the woodland caribou wearing it in darker tones. A gray-brown body and face, white neck and tail, brown nose, ears, and legs with white fetlocks and feet of ebony is the general style, although there are many variations. Calves are a spotless ruddy brown. The orange antlers are palmated in greatly varying degree. The mountain caribou is yet another, though not very numerous, kind, living in the Rockies of Canada and southern Alaska, much of the time above timberline. It is even bigger than the woodland animal and darkest of all, being nearly black.

The smallest, shortest-legged caribou, the barren-ground variety, are nevertheless by far the most migratory. In autumn they may meet

the woodland caribou where the forest gives up growing in the face of Arctic winds, but they never mingle with them. They have come in swarming wedge-shaped herds of many thousands, close packed as sheep, to eat the moss and lichens which farther north are buried too deep in snow for even such cold country beasts to dig to.

They manage well enough in moderately heavy snow, scooping with their forefeet; and it is possible that that part of their antlers which projects just over their noses is used as a crust cutter when one is needed. But after mid-September they are likely to find the larder all too tightly locked by old King Boreas himself, and the long march south begins without delay.

But as soon as the weather will allow, they hurry north again, clear to the bogs by the shores of the Arctic Sea, where swamp plants and seaweed offer an interesting menu. Here by the icy ocean, in May or early June, each caribou cow will bear her calf in as private a spot as she can find in that wide, open region of the world. The birthplace often is in a still unmelted bank of snow. The mother never leaves her young one, for like her ruminating cousin in the same cruel country, the musk-ox, she must keep a constant watch against the wolves. For that matter, hiding places are hard to find, even from the everlasting and lambasting wind.

In about two hours the calf can stumble along at its mother's heels, and in a week is trotting ably with her everywhere, even swimming ice water lakes and streams close by her side. By the beginning of September it is weaned and eating moss and ready for the southward journey. Each little band of cows and calves joins others as the trek goes on, feeding morning and evening, moving onward all day long, fifty or sixty miles from dawn to dusk.

As winter pursues them, prodding them on with icicle goad, they travel still more rapidly, and sleep on the ice of frozen lakes when they can for more security from ever hungrier wolves. The bulls in growing herds are coming too, but sometimes days behind. At the approach of storms and blizzards, they are not distressed but, on the contrary, often are inspired to do a circle dance, whirling round and round in sheer enjoyment of hard whistling winds and driving snow.

Once all have reached the wintering ground, the yearly bull fights start in earnest. Though they make no wallows, caribou and reindeer bulls in mating time become the strongest smelling of all male deer the whole world over, even muskier than moose. They are the hardest, most persistent fighters, though their antlers are perhaps the most brittle, so that portions are frequently broken off. Successful contenders, by endless effort, may assemble harems of a dozen cows, but in the process, lasting about three weeks, they practically forget to eat. When the rows are over and all is peace among them, they desire nothing but to rest and eat, and eat some more. Winter comes and goes, and with it go the caribou to the barren-grounds again.

Unlike other deer, these cold country creatures wear soft, short hair all over their muzzles. And unlike other female deer, reindeer and caribou cows have antlers, smaller than the bulls', not used for dueling, but added armament against attack by bears, wolves, wolverines, and wildcats. Of these enemies the wolves are much the worst. Very numerous in the north, they are not so dangerous in summertime or early fall. Then they feed on smaller fry such as lemmings and other rodents, hunting alone or in little family groups. But as the cold increases these groups join with each other to stalk musk-oxen and caribou, and are very hard to cope with.

Bulls shed their antlers around January, but fortunately the cows carry their weapons all winter, the time of greatest danger, and the time too when they are carrying the unborn future caribou or reindeer of the world. Once the weather and their enemies ease off, so do their no longer needed antlers.

In Alaska, and all the portions of Canada, from the northern limit of trees to the borders of the United States, the bigger woodland caribou is found, its range very nearly the same as that of the moose. There used to be woodland caribou in the Adirondacks, and not long ago there still were some in northern Maine. But the only ones outside of zoos left in this country now are a few in Minnesota.

REINDEER AND CARIBOU

Since they are such ultra-northern animals, the nearest most of us may ever come to seeing caribou will be at that moment when imaginary reindeer pause with Santa's sleigh each Christmas Eve, upon our snow-clad housetops. If we should hear the clickety-click of castanets instead of the jingling of small bells, we might believe the animals were really there.

Pronghorn Fencing

PRONGHORN ANTELOPE
OR PRONGBUCK

NOW for a few pages you are in for some pretty puzzling paragraphs. For they are going to deal with the puzzle of the prongbuck's horns. These are hollow and braced by bony spikes like other horns; but they branch like antlers and are shed every year, instead of growing continuously from the head as with all other antelopes, goats, sheep, and cattle.

It is plain, on examining a prongbuck's cast-off horn, that it is made of many hairs all glued together by a strong cementing gelatin. This gelatin is secreted by the skin which encloses the bony spikes like velvet on a growing antler. The hairs of this velvet grow, as the cement, exuded from the same skin, flows and hardens all about them, the two together forming horn.

The process starts at the tips of the spikes inside the old horns, which are themselves no longer growing, held to the head and inner spikes only by the old dead hairs of the year before. The spikes are encased in velvet concealed within the old horns. The topmost velvet, with exuding cement, hardens and forms the sharp points of new horns that are to be. The velvet skin, inside the old horns but enveloping the spikes, continues building horn and pushing it upward, like a new nail growing under an old one. This steady upward thrusting continually breaks the old dead hairs still anchoring the old dead horns, till presently, with a sudden shake

Just before shedding | Just after | Later: Velvet all gone | Prongs beginning | New set complete

of the head or a knock against a branch or rock, the last attachment breaks and off they come.

This discloses the new black tips and the rest of the spikes still in their velvet covering. Steadily from the new tips downward the nature of this covering changes from a hairy to a horny substance, as cementing gelatin is secreted. After all the velvet has turned into horn, more horn of the same hair and gelatin kind still forms and pushes upward from the skin at the base of the spikes, at the same time producing on each horn the branch or prong. Thus, when finished, the horns are twelve to twenty inches long, far longer than the dagger spikes they sheath. The prongs which started at their bases stop moving up when halfway to the tips.

Through September and October, the new weapons serve the selfsame purpose that antlers do the deer, preventing, through combat, all but the best bucks from fathering the next year's fawns. In these bouts some of the finest fencing and swordplay of the ruminant world is exhibited. The prong is used exactly like a sword or dagger guard, stopping and helping to parry the adversary's thrust, giving the buck an instant's hold while he sets himself to shift ground suddenly as he tries to gash his rival's throat. If the prongs of the rival fail to stop the stroke, swift side-stepping still can save him from a fierce and sometimes fatal slashing.

The horns are turned on coyotes and other enemies for the safety of all, as long as they are serviceable. Females have little three-inch horns which sometimes come in handy, but since they don't indulge in duels with others of their kind they have no prongs or dagger guards. As with almost all the deer and antelope, hoof work is the ever-ready method of defense. Prongbucks kill snakes as whitetails do, by leaping and landing on them with all ninety or one hundred pounds concentrated in four sharp hoofs held close together.

Prongbucks have good hearing and efficient sniffers, but trust mostly to their eyes, which are probably the finest of all four-footed animals. They will watch with ease the movements of a coyote so far away that a man must use high-powered field glasses to make him out at all. Dwellers on plain and prairie for millions of years, where stalking enemies can be seen long before they are heard or even scented, prongbucks think in terms of sight much more than sound or smell.

Thus, if a hunting animal tries to sneak up close enough to rush and spring, they worry little as long as they can watch him, being able to outrun all natural enemies. As he moves up, trying to hide behind each rise of ground, brush clump, or gully wall, they countermove to keep him well in view. Not to know his exact whereabouts is unnerving. To see him is not to be surprised. That is the age-old axiom which has always worked in dealing with the beasts of prey and Indians. Today they generally do not linger so tantalizingly near their stalking human enemies, for they have learned that the bark of a rifle may mean injury from a long way off.

This habit of looking hard and long at things accounts for their reputation for insatiable curiosity. For seeing something is not enough unless it is understood as well. A strange object must be observed at ever closer quarters until its nature is established in their minds. Thus in the old days a man could hang a handkerchief on a bush and hide till prongbucks, seesawing cautiously ever closer, came near enough at last for him to fire.

White hunters probably learned this trick
from Indians, but it will not work any more.
Prongbucks understand more of human ways
than once they did. It used to be that they
wouldn't jump a barbed wire range fence only
four feet high, but now they do. They wouldn't
even jump a railroad track when first the steel
was stretched across the west. But their fears
were overcome because of an odd trait they have
regarding racing. The speed of a train looked
like a challenge to them, and often they took it
up. But their idea of winning a race is to run
parallel to the challenger, whoever he happens
to be, edging ever closer. Then, in a terrific
burst of speed, they delight to cross in front of
him and tear away leaving him to lumber along
in their dust.

At this the engineer in the "iron horse" may
have grinned a little (they could outrun the
early railroad trains), but more than one horse-
man, mocked in this manner, may have felt a

momentary dissatisfaction with the best he could get out of his straining steed. For long distances the prongbucks, fastest of all four-footed animals in America, and possibly the world, can keep up a clip of forty-five miles per hour, but in sprints they get up to fifty-five and maybe more. At least one has crossed in front of an automobile racing it at fifty miles an hour. To do this it would need a speed of nearly a mile a minute!

They rarely run more than a few miles away from anything that frightens them. They almost always circle back for, like whitetails, they love the land that lies around the spot where they were born. They only leave it if the food gives out. Of course, in the northern part of their range they have to change from summer to winter quarters, sometimes migrating as much as one hundred and fifty miles, though usually far fewer.

In olden times, west of the Mississippi, there

were millions of them wherever there was fairly level open land, constant companions of the bison herds. For prongbucks are grazers, browsing only if there is no grass, though eating cactus in the driest regions where they live. When cattle came into the country they followed them as they had the buffalo, thus getting up into higher grazing grounds and passing through timbered land to do so. Without these heavier, hollow-horned relatives to lead them, all probably would have remained down on the plain. They do not care much for forests or high mountains, and they don't enjoy snow, though they are found all the way from Mexico up into Canada.

Prongbucks are best suited to semi-arid regions, where running rarely brings them onto boggy ground. Like horses, they long ago dispensed with the little back toes of their hoofs, since these are only useful in soft going and contribute nothing to their speed. "The fewer his toes, the faster he goes" has always been the rule, and the flying feet of a prongbuck only seem to flick the ground, not really tread upon it, the legs almost as blurred as the spokes of a whirling buggy wheel.

Prongbucks are three feet high at the shoulders, and the principal body color is tan. They have black horns, hoofs, and eyes, with black on their noses, under the ears, and sometimes on the mane. There are bars of white on the throat, and their chops and chests are white, as are their undersides and rumps. The hair on the latter stands on end in fear and excitement and acts as a splendid signal of alarm to others at a distance, as well as furnishing a flag for fleeing fawns to follow.

White, since it throws off all the sun's rays, is brighter and carries farther than any other color. One might expect black to be visible a long way, but it absorbs light rays and atmosphere dims it down. Thus white is a color often seen on the rears of many animals whose habit is to run for their lives, such as rabbits and many ruminants. The rump patch of the prongbuck is a reflector of the very best, and when the hairs are all on end they seem to intensify the light-throwing power.

Such a long range warning signal system is most useful in the great open spaces where prongbucks live. The mother hides her unspot-

Disc hair up and down

ted fawns (twins usually), as does a deer, in brush or dry grass, which their tan coats so resemble. Or in the southwest deserts she may cloister them in separate cactus clumps. Like a deer she leads enemies far from her odorless young ones, or fights if she must as best she can. By the time the youngsters are ten days old, they can gallop off with her and leave a lot of troubles behind, but in a few weeks even wolves can't catch them.

For a long time though, so many bullets caught up with prongbucks that their millions had been reduced to a very few thousand some forty years ago. Hunting them had to be regulated as with so many other things, and they have increased to about one hundred and fifty thousand animals. It looks now as though the prongbuck, fleetest of all four-footed Americans, will survive and live long in our lucky land.

MOUNTAIN "GOAT"

HARD as it may be to believe, the other
kind of American antelope is really an
antelope and not a goat, though in
habits and the possession of a beard it so re-
sembles one. Besides the beard, the outline of
the miscalled mountain "goat" is quite mislead-
ing because of its long white overcoat of hair

which covers its soft woolen underwear, being so thick on rump and shoulders as to make the animal look sway-backed, which it is not.

This is the only ruminant which is normally pure white throughout the year, except, of course, for its hoofs and horns. The latter, worn by both sexes, are a shiny black and, though short, are skewer-sharp, excellent for changing the minds of high ranging wolves, bears, or mountain lions, or of eagles which sometimes try to snatch the kids or fawns.

At these altitudes the eagle's attack from the air may not come very much above the goats' own level. On their landward side they never expect any trouble at all from above, four-legged enemies customarily coming up from timberline far below. So they ignore the cliffs and crags above them while basking in small family groups on some sunny southward-facing slope.

A hunter, taking the long way around and up behind the peak where he has seen them, can finally look over and down on their unsuspecting ease. But like as not, while he has been exerting himself to near exhaustion, his heart laboring heavily and every breath an effort in the high thin air, the half dozen living snowdrifts may have finished their siesta and gone to graze upon another mountain.

These true antelopes of America stay in the highest Rockies of some northwestern states, where blizzards are the rule and snow is usually in evidence. They live at ever lower levels as their range runs northward into colder Canada and Alaska, gleaning a good living from the scanty, dry, tough little mountain mosses, where any other beast would starve if it didn't freeze first. These antelopes do not run swiftly and are not especially able rock jumpers, but as climbers they are perhaps the most sure-footed things in all the world, a great two hundred pound "goat" going up steep slippery granite where a man could barely find a fingerhold.

Only once in a blue moon do they miss their footing and fall. Even then, so artful are they in tumbling without tension and in gaining new footholds farther down, that falls are seldom fatal. Often in their kidhood they play a game of tumbledown on some steep rock that ends in a safe wide ledge, and that practice stands them in good stead when real falls come.

They know all about land, rock, and snow slides. For the most part they live above the worst of these, especially in the spring, the season of most danger. But, if caught in the path of a slide, they climb or jump to some safe point and watch it pass or pile up where they have just been standing. The adults may grunt hoarsely in excitement and the kids may bleat, but rarely are they harmed by nature's great rampages.

During the long snowbound seasons of their chilly haunts, these great "goats" are all but invisible at a little distance because of their white wool. But as summer melts the mountains' whiteness, they become conspicuous against a granite background. Yet so slow to shrink are the lingering drifts, that even in midsummer one may mistake a resting animal for a heap of snow. Then when he moves about his dizzy, dangerous domain, you will see a living snow-drift drifting. With this last look let us leave him and the other antelope and deer to the enjoyment of their interesting lives in the vast and varied regions of the wilderness.

The End